The
Undercurrent
A Journey to Purpose

Anita L. Proctor

Contents

Acknowledgements

I want to first give thanks to Jesus Christ, my Lord and Savior. Because of Christ, I am no longer bound by fear in its entirety, especially the fear of rejection and the fear of the opinions of others. I am a new creation in Him. I never would have made it this far in the journey if He had not come into my life to do a complete work. Thank You Jesus, for saving me!

To my husband, my friend, and my biggest support system, thank you for always pushing me to be the best me. You always encourage me with a thumbs up, "good job" or "go for it and do your thing" (smile) and I appreciate that so much. I value your confidence in me when I lacked confidence within myself. Thank you for keeping me balanced with jokes and laughter, reminding me to not sweat the small stuff and keep it moving. Love you boo.

To my beautiful daughters Keishawna Renee' and Jocelyn Marie', mommy's cheerleaders. You have no idea how much your words of encouragement and wisdom along my journey kept me moving forward. You two were my reason for living and striving to be the best mother I knew to be throughout the years. Now you are both mothers and I have already seen that you are a blessing to your little ones. I pray God's favor over you both. Love you always my treasured jewels!

To my son-in-law, thank you for all your love and support. I know the best is yet to come for you in your journey. Stay focused on Jesus and He will lead the way, love Mom.

To my bonus daughter, Sherrie, my ray of sunshine! Thank you for allowing me to be a part of your life. You truly are a joy and blessing to our family. Thank you for being a part of my push squad (lol). You really were a blessing in disguise. Love you much, mom.

To my parents, thank you for never ceasing to love me, even in my mess. I am a product of love, because of you. You instilled in me the value of people and never judging a book by its cover. You taught me the significance of having a relationship with Jesus Christ and ensuring I taught the same values to my children. Thank you for your example of faith in God and faithfulness to God. Love you mommy and daddy.

Special thanks to Tia and Letrice for not only being my friends, but my sisters in Christ, and my prayer partners. You two have inspired me to always walk in who God created me to be, to never be confined by the box I put myself in, or allow others to put me in. You have prayed for me, spoken life over me, and pulled the best out of me, in more ways than one. Words cannot express my gratitude to you both. Love and appreciate you from a grateful heart.

To all my family, sister/friends, and CPBBC family, thank you for your prayers, support, and right on time words: as they were truly needed and appreciated.

To my Pastors, whom I love soooooo much!!! You are more than Pastors to me. You are a second set of parents and I am truly grateful to be one of your daughters in ministry. Your ministry saved my life, propelled me to soar and spread my wings. There is no doubt in my mind that God placed me under your leadership, but also in your hearts. Thank you for praying, speaking life, teaching me the foundational truths of God's word, and loving me unconditionally, "as is."

Forward

I am so excited that my sister-friend has birthed such an amazing and awe-inspiring masterpiece! This is not just an ordinary book. It is a life-changer! I have had the privilege of sharing some of Rev. Anita's journey and I know first-hand of her love for God and desire to see others set free, healed, and delivered. I believe this book will answer many questions as to *why* we often feel stuck and unable to move forward into all the great things God has planned for our lives. It truly challenged me in areas where I needed to change and be set free! Rev. Anita does a masterful job of taking you through the process of exposing those things that lie beneath the surface. Through her practical examples, down-to-earth personality, reflection questions, and her own personal struggles, she brings you to a place of freedom and intimacy with God. I believe *The Undercurrent* will speak to you wherever you are on your life's journey and will truly transform and propel you into the person you were always destined to be! *–Rev. Letrice Weaver, Author and President, Shine 4 Him Ministries*

The Undercurrent is a must-read book that took me on a journey that compelled me to see myself through the eyes of the Father.

Rev. Anita's words in this book are masterfully written. To watch her journey and her impact on the lives of her family, ministry and friends has been a divine set up by God! Her walk with God is proof that He is into transforming lives from the inside out. The transformation of Rev. Anita's life and ministry displays how His surgical hands can go beneath the surface to bring us into the place He has called us to be. This book takes you on a journey of discovery that will lead you into an intimate relationship with the Lord. Don't worry! As you are reading this book, it will feel as though Rev. Anita is taking you by the hand and walking with you through the process to uncover the real you. Take the dive to go deeper! - *Rev. Tia Collins*

Introduction

"For I know the thoughts and plans that I have for you,
says the Lord, thoughts and plans for welfare and peace
and not for evil, to give you hope in your final outcome."
- Jeremiah 29:11 (AMP)

Have you ever wondered why am I here? What is my purpose in life? Do I even have a purpose or was I just meant to exist, live, and then die? Believe it or not, we all have a purpose in life and every experience or moment is tied to that purpose. What I did not know is on the path of discovery to purpose, hidden things would begin to surface. These were things I really did not want to deal with, let alone talk about it. But God will not allow us to stay in a place of obscurity, as our story is not our own. It is about freeing someone else from a place of brokenness.

So often we have our own thoughts and plans for our lives, not realizing the Creator of all things has mapped out plans for us all along. But many of us go throughout our life's journey assuming we know what we want our outcome to be in life. The reality of that thought process is that it is unfortunately based upon certain moments or events that made lasting impressions in our hearts and shaped the way we think about ourselves, people, and life as a whole. However, when we discover there have been recurring cycles or instances that paralyzed us, and even hindered us from reaching our full potential or experiencing the fullness of joy and peace, it is at that moment we will begin to embrace all that He has for us. It is at that moment that we fully grasp Romans 8:28 as it says, "We are assured and know that [God being a partner in their labor] all things work together and are [fitting into a plan] for good to and for those who love God and are called according to [His] design and purpose." (Amplified Classic Version)

When we come to a complete understanding that we are called according to His design and His purpose, then we can rest inwardly knowing the outcome will be great. It is at that moment that the raging river of inner turmoil can cease, and we can begin to flow in the current of God's Holy Spirit. We can then be consumed by an inward peace that will surpass our understanding and truly enjoy the journey to purpose.

The purpose of this book is to encourage those of you who may have experienced life-altering events, tragedy, devastation, and hurt beyond articulation, that regardless of the situation, and whatever has happened, know you are still destined for a divine purpose. In sharing pieces of my journey, my heart's desire is that this book provokes something in you to open up and receive the healing power of God.

For it is only through His healing power that you can discover your life has been predestined by God for greatness. In spite of what the enemy meant for evil, God knew the plans He had, and it all works out for your good. Let this book encourage you to get up, live, and start your journey to discovering your true purpose in life......lives are waiting on you.

CHAPTER 1

Beneath the Surface

"The heart is deceitful above all things, and desperately wicked; Who can know it?" - Jeremiah 17:9 (NKJV)

Have you ever wondered why you do what you do? Why do you overreact or respond negatively or have a pessimistic outlook? Have you ever asked yourself, "What's wrong with me? Why can't I ever finish what I started? Why do certain situations or challenges affect me this way? Why do certain things cause me to have sleepless nights? Why do I draw the same type of people into my circle? What voids do they fill for me? When I am in a decision-making moment, why do I experience overwhelming anxiety or fear?" It is as if you find yourself going back and forth in your mind with the 'what if's.' What if this happens? What if that happens? What if it does not work out? What if I fail? What if I am rejected? You go through all of that "analysis paralysis" only to learn after the decision is made, it was not as bad as you thought.

Or maybe you have been put in an uncomfortable situation, where the expectations of people cause you to feel an inexplicable amount of pressure to perform and to be something you were never intended to be in life. This pressure can cause you to feel like the walls of your chest are caving in. The irritation or frustration becomes insurmountable and fits of outburst take you w-a-a-a-y-y-y out of character. Or perhaps you have been pulled in many directions filling the voids or needs of others, all the while neglecting your right to say "no." Or you could be distracted by staying busy to keep you from having to look in the mirror.

These are real-life moments many of us have experienced at some point in time. The problem with all of this is we fail to stop in life to ponder, reflect, and seek out the answers to our many questions, quirks, issues, and challenges in life. Sometimes we start to pause, but then we quickly move on to the next moment until something else occurs, which reminds us of our former experiences, and we find ourselves reacting in the same manner without any change. The definition of insanity is repeating the same actions over and over again but expecting different results or a different outcome.

Before we can move towards the fulfillment of our true purpose, we have to allow God to show us the root or roots that hinder our progress in the journey. Yes, you may very well continue in your journey, eventually reaching the intended destination, but without going through the process, the question is will you encounter complete joy, peace, and freedom that can accompany you along the way to destiny? I dare to say no, not until you address the undercurrents beneath the surface of your heart; the undercurrents that can delay your progression and growth within the process.

The Undercurrents

An undercurrent is "a type of current that runs below the surface of the water. The direction of the undercurrent goes in the opposite direction of the surface currents." Now depending on the water conditions, the strength of the undercurrent can vary. Another definition of an undercurrent is "an underlying feeling or influence, especially one that is contrary to the prevailing atmosphere and is not expressed openly." In other words, there is a resistance happening beneath the surface, not always visible for all to see. This resistance is taking place in our hearts and can go undetected until something or someone decides to jump in to disrupt the calm exterior waters of our life. It is at that point we along with others discover there are some underlying issues that we are unable to suppress. The resistance or opposition, called a defense mechanism, can be the result of unresolved hurt, fears, disappointment, anger, resentment, even bitterness that has gone unchecked for years. Unfortunately, the opposition does not rise and expose itself until the waters are disturbed unexpectedly. What I have learned (and still learning) is that you can literally go through life coping with the hidden secrets of your past and believing that your outward success is an indication of true freedom. Unfortunately, my friend, that is an untruth.

So, Don't Be Fooled...

Believe it or not, we can be fooled by what we look like on the outside. We may have a successful career, some of us are financially stable, some of us are married with two kids and a dog and living in a house with a white picket fence. Or we are single, at the height of our career, living large and appearing to have it all together. We're living with no visible signs of trouble. We are maintaining a sense of normalcy, thinking we are powerful and in control of life. Oh, how contrary that is from the truth. We live in a false perception of what the "good life" is when our inner reality does not correspond or mirror our outer performance stage. We function as if all is well, believing certain things do not affect us anymore. We oftentimes take the stance, "I have moved on or I am not even thinking about that anymore," when we know the truth of that statement.

The Warning Signs

The strength of an undercurrent can vary, depending on the surrounding conditions of the water. I live in the DMV (Washington, D.C.-Maryland-Virginia) area, near the Potomac River. On a hot summer day, this river, for example, gives the illusion to many people, that it is okay to jump in and take a swim. There are many warning signs all around, "Do Not Go Swimming! Dangerous! Rough Waters!" Yet and still people ignore the warning signs and still jump in to take a swim. The river appears inviting and calm on the surface level, but people quickly discover the deception of the river. They find themselves drowning and oftentimes unable to be rescued. This is because there was not only an undercurrent way too strong to resist, but there was unseen debris, branches, trees, and whatever else that became entangled in the flow of the river. Not to mention this river is also highly toxic with bacteria that comes from the run-over from heavy rains and the garbage from age-old sewage pipes that date back to the 1860s. They fill and overflow into the canals and then into the river. Just like the Potomac River, we too can give people an illusion that our life is welcoming and pleasantly calm on the surface. But that is until people get too close and discover a hidden truth, that there is not only debris from our past but toxic behavior that pollutes or taints those who come in close proximity. They, unfortunately, missed our warning signs. They missed how guarded we tried to be. They missed our passive-aggressive behavior. They missed our nasty ways. They missed our inconsistent ways. There were multiple signs and red flags, but people missed them because we mastered how to hide our truth.

It's Time....

It's time to do some cleaning, some repairing, some digging, some uprooting, some opening and some closing within our hearts. Throughout the process of this journey to purpose, you will need to decide to deal with the old, in order to establish the new. Like the old sewage pipes of Washington, DC, which are WELL overdue of an overhaul, some of you are well overdue for a reconstruction. It's time for the river within to flow without the hidden debris that can restrict movement on the predestined path set before you were formed in your mother's womb. It's time to deal with the root cause of defiance so there can be a free-flowing river within. There is a root, an origination, a source, or a starting point to everything that grows. Allow God to show you the origin of the anxiety/worry, the root cause of fear in all of its forms (rejection, failure, success, and people), the source of anger, bitterness, and resentment, the source of the jealousy, sarcastic attitude, pessimistic mindset, and anything that keeps you stuck in a time, an era, or causes you to have a negative response to unexpected challenges. It is vital to get to the root of a thing. Before we decide to go to the doctor when we are not well, we experience some symptoms, not truly knowing the source of our ailment. We go to the doctor because we are limited in our medical knowledge and skill (that's for my Google doctors). It's after the doctor begins to ask us a series of questions based upon those symptoms, that he or she can then provide the appropriate diagnosis and treat the problem. God is the Chief Physician in our lives and as we begin or continue on our journey, we have to first allow Him to reveal what has been hidden.

For us to be used for God's glory, we have to sometimes revisit our story, the journey of how we evolved into who we are today. We must come to grips with the fact that some moments in our lives were traumatizing, almost paralyzing to the point of no movement. Those traumatic experiences did happen and were not a figment of our imagination. The moment did reshape how we interacted with other people and even related to God Himself.

In my own journey, I discovered what the enemy meant for evil, God truly turned it around for my good. I learned the key to living with a constant and calm flow above and beneath the surface. I have not only learned to rest in the presence of God, but I now have a true relationship with the King of kings and Lord of lords, Jesus Christ. It is in His presence where I can be open and honest about what I prefer to dismiss and move on from. But I also learned that apart from God, I could do nothing on my own. I was just suppressing the pain and hoping the memories would just disappear. But the reality of it all was it caused me to do more damage to myself than good. All because I would not take the necessary steps, I needed in order to heal completely. So, I encourage you, take the time you need and begin to heal.

A TIME OF REFLECTION

Over the next few chapters, be open, pause often, reflect, and allow cleansing to take place. Allow things to be revealed that you may have suppressed, ignored, or attempted to act as if it did not affect you in any way. Pray and ask God to bring to your remembrance certain events or moments that began shaping your identity that may be opposite of the identity God ordained for you to walk in. Whatever lies beneath the surface where surrounding conditions have hindered you in moving forward…. it's time to deal with it.

Here are a few questions to ask yourself:

1. Why do I react when this _____occurs? (fill in the blank)

2. What is beneath the surface of my heart I have chosen not to deal with?

3. Have I prevented God from beginning the healing process?

CHAPTER 2

Hidden Truth

"And you will know the truth, and the truth will set you free." - John 8:32 (ESV)

In the Merriam-Webster dictionary, the word hidden means, "being out of sight, not readily apparent, concealed, unexplained, undisclosed or secret." If we are honest, many of us have lived or are still living in a place of hiddenness, a place of secrets, an undisclosed place where no one knows the location. It can be like living behind a fortress. A fortress is a "military stronghold, a place not susceptible to outside influence or disturbance." It is a barrier to protect what is within from what is on the outside. If the truth be told, you may have felt like this was the only way to protect yourself from the enemy who came in and stole from you once, maybe even twice, but you made up in your mind, never again will I allow myself to be vulnerable, unprotected, or open to any type of attack. When we go into the hiding place within, we become guarded, suspicious, and leery of anyone or anything that resembles the enemy that caused a breach in our security system. We begin to toughen our armor, build our defenses, strengthen our artillery, and attempt to sharpen our intel and insight just in case, so nothing will catch us off guard. The pain we felt was far too deep to allow ourselves to go through that ever again. But, when God comes into your life, all that is hidden, all that is secret, all that is undisclosed, and all that is pushed down and buried begin to resurface, and the plan of avoidance is no longer available.

The Source

If we are to press onward in life, then those things we were so great at avoiding, will need to be confronted. The band-aid we applied attempting to cover those things needs to be removed, so the stench of our gaping wound can properly heal. I know all too well about suppressing and hiding pain. I hid my truth for over 22 years. Even though my life appeared to be moving outwardly, my life actually paused inwardly starting in the summer of 1980. I was nine years old and just finished up the third grade, when I was sexually molested by a family member. It was a memory that took me from the age of 31, when I disclosed the secret to my parents, to the age of 45, to be completely and supernaturally healed by God. For 22 years, I was stuck at age 9 inwardly, but for 14 years, I slowly allowed God in to heal me. Let me be clear though, it does not have to take that long for you to receive your healing. I truly believe the healing process is dependent upon an individual's level of openness to God doing the inward work and a willingness to let go and let God.

Cause and Effect

This moment in time was the beginning of a tumultuous childhood that no child should ever have to encounter. I had no idea until years later, that my innocence, my identity, my voice, and even my rational thinking was stolen from me that very day. I did not know then what I know now, and that is, God clearly had grand plans for my life. I know, because the devil was determined to steal, kill, and destroy me early by coming after me in the same way on numerous occasions up until I was 12 years old, by not just one person, but several others. He attempted to prevent me from knowing who I was destined to be. The enemy's whole plan was to steal my ability to see what God saw when He created me…I was predestined for GREATNESS! The enemy peeked into my future and sent a vicious attack to stop me, to kill my ability to freely receive and give the love God intended for me. He attempted to destroy my ability to experience what real intimacy was like. He tried to distort my view of what a true relationship with God is supposed to look like. He attempted to hold me hostage to my memories of fear and feeling unprotected.

This life-altering experience was the beginning of many years of struggling to be the real me or even know what the real me looked like through the eyes of God. Those three years of my childhood life were meant to stop the fullness of my potential. So, the enemy thought. I will not lie to you, I had to overcome A LOT. The experience made me very much afraid of everything, even afraid of people. It caused me to think I was not good enough, inadequate, incompetent, and unworthy to experience love the way God designed it to be. I believed I was unattractive and truthfully speaking, I felt like damaged goods. The violation of my innocence planted many seeds that tainted the view I had of myself from grade school up to adulthood. However, no one would know it, because I was good at performing and wearing the right mask at the right time. I will discuss the different masks we learn to wear in the next chapter.

Open Your Mouth

In my journey of revealing and healing, I needed to let it out. I think it is important to speak your truth to someone, a trustworthy person, of course, do not just tell anyone. As for me, I needed to begin breaking down the fortress I had built around my heart, around my love, around my life. I did not realize the fortress was not only keeping others from hurting me again, but I was also hindering God from fully healing me, which ultimately was hurting me. If I could not let my guard down, I could not let God come in to do surgery and mend my broken heart. God is not going to go against our will. A relationship is about being vulnerable with the one who loves you unconditionally. So, it is imperative, to be honest about not only what took place, but what you felt in the aftermath of the trauma. So often we sugarcoat our real feelings and emotions for fear of judgment or ridicule from people who want to tell you how you should feel about what happened to you. Let me encourage you from a person who has "been there and done that"…let it all out - the shame and even the guilt, because God already knows. That's the funny part about it… He is very much aware of all your emotions that range from anger to resentment to unforgiveness. He already knows!!! So be honest with Him and whomever God allows you to confide in.

It is important to know that the opposition to keep things hidden is spiritual warfare. This is not a war from without against people, but a war from within. It is a war against the lies of the enemy, the lie that this is a private matter, that it happened so long ago and not worth revisiting, the lie that this is too hard to overcome, and the lie that this is just who you are and it's too late to change. It is never too late to heal and it's never too late to change, but you do have to want to heal and want to change.

You may not have been sexually abused as a child. You may have had an absentee parent in your life, been bullied as a child, involved in a devastating accident, experienced a traumatizing divorce, or betrayal by a friend, but whatever the case, know that deliverance and free-dom is attainable. You can live the abundant life not just outwardly, but inwardly too. Remember, whatever the enemy attempts to do, he can never succeed in his plan when you come out of the place, he thought would keep you forever. I am a living witness. As you can see, as I write my story, this is my proof that he did not succeed. So, let this encourage you to keep going through the process of revealing and healing so you can come out on the other side to your purpose.

A TIME OF REFLECTION

Take some time to sit quietly and reflect back to when the fortress was built on the inside; when you first made the decision to hide the truth of things that caused deep hurt. Healing is a process. By no means should you expect an overnight change. It takes work on your part to let go and give it over to God once and for all. But, if you are willing, God is capable.

In your quiet time, ask yourself the following questions:

1. What am I running from in my past that I know I need to address?

2. Who can I talk to that is trustworthy and will not judge my honest emotions, but not allow me to stay in that place? (Note: you need positive, compassionate reinforcements through this process).

3. Am I willing to take the necessary steps to open up and let God into the secret place of my heart?

CHAPTER 3

Remove the Mask

"O Lord, you search me, and you know me. You know when I sit and when I rise; You discern my thoughts from afar; You search out my path and my lying down and are acquainted with all my ways." - Psalm 139:1-3 (ESV)

Now that we have exposed the hidden truth of our past, we must now begin the process of unmasking. Masks are our disguises, façades, and defense mechanisms that we form to conceal the truth of our emotional reality. Our past trauma and earth-shattering moments in life can cause us to learn how to adapt to certain environments to prepare us for any unforeseen danger that may occur. It is our way of protecting ourselves and building those fortresses or barriers, that I discussed in chapter 2. We put them on based upon the given situation that presents itself. We learn how to "front" before others and pretend that we are okay. The disturbing piece of this is that some of us are really good at putting up façades. A façade is the art of becoming who you need to be depending upon who is in your space at the time. The problem is after functioning with all of these different masks for so long, you begin to lose sight of who you are really supposed to be. Why? Because it was easier to repress, restrain, and cover the agony, than to release it, surrender it, and get help in order to be restored.

Exposed

The challenge with wearing a mask is that a person with any level of discernment can see through that false exterior; especially those who used to wear that same type of mask. Remember the saying, "it takes one to know one." You are exposed without even knowing you have been detected as a "pretender." We think we are great actresses or actors and we actually should receive an academy award for some of our best performances. The funny part is you really believe in your mind you have folks fooled. But, the hidden truth of that notion is not only can others see behind that front, God, can see it all. Whether you realize it or not, God is familiar with "all" of your ways. He knows the very number of hairs on our head. Nothing is a secret to God when it comes to our so-called camouflage. He is the Creator, and He knows His creation. He knows because He is omniscient, meaning He is all-knowing. In Matthew 9:4 it says, "But Jesus knew what they were thinking…" So, wearing a mask and putting up a line of defense serves no purpose other than providing you a false sense of protection.

How It Started....

I first learned how to put on a mask from those who were used as pawns in the scheme of the enemy, when I was told not to tell. I was told, "if you tell your parents, they will be mad at you." This by far was a lie from the pit of hell. But those very words still planted a seed of rejection. I had to learn at nine years old how to hide how I really felt. I had to bottle up my tears, my thoughts of not feeling secure and safe when I was alone, and the rage that grew inside towards those who violated my innocence. Even though my dad was an outstanding police officer, this was one case he could not crack. I worked hard at the art of hiding, almost believing I was invisible, even in a crowded room. I suppressed my voice when I sensed I was in trouble. I could literally be quiet for hours and not speak when questioned by my parents. I remember as a teenager, I ran away because I got in trouble for something my little brother did...well, I was partly responsible. Nevertheless, when I returned home later that evening, (yeah, I didn't run far or too long...lol), I saw the pain I caused my parents, and I immediately shut down internally. This was something I had crafted. I was good at silence. So much so, my mom asked a psychiatrist friend of hers to talk to me that night and even they could not crack my code. I trained myself to go to a place where I could not hear or see those around me. After two hours of them sitting there questioning me and responding with complete silence, they gave up and told my mom to pray.

If They Only Knew....

So many people, like myself, go through life with so much inner turmoil that constantly gnaws at them. If people had x-ray vision, they would be in amazement with what other people have buried deep down beneath the surface. People put up these façades to prevent connection and trusting others again. This disguise prevents our ability to be vulnerable and transparent because showing others our true selves can make us fearful of displaying flaws, imperfections, inadequacies, and shortcomings. By doing so, this gives way to our fear of not being valued, loved as is, viewed as significant, or worth protecting.

Defense Mechanisms

So now I want to talk about our defense mechanisms, how they show up in our lives, and how others are affected when they are on display. A defense mechanism is "a mental process (repression or progression) initiated, typically unconsciously, to avoid conscious conflict or anxiety." In other words, it is the process to keep hidden, an internal emotional wound. When the environment around us is not conducive to our inward atmosphere then our natural inclination is to safeguard or shield our heart from further damage. The very thing that emerges as our defense, is also the very thing that blocks our wounds from being healed completely. It prevents the light of Christ from coming into our dark places.

Identify Your Mechanism

According to a Healthline article by Kimberly Holland, titled "10 Defense Mechanisms: What are They and How They Help Us Cope," she states, "Defense mechanisms are behaviors people use to separate themselves from unpleasant events, actions, or thoughts. These psychological strategies may help put distance between themselves and threats or unwanted feelings, such as guilt or shame." When I read this, I was so amazed, because it explained why I would go into my silent place. I was trying to separate myself from experiencing another threat that would cause me to deal with those unwanted feelings of torment. To help you along in your process of unmasking and exposing those areas, I want to share just a few defense mechanisms from the article, as I believe it is the truth that brings freedom.

1. **Denial** – When we refuse to accept reality or facts. This is the most common defense mechanism for most of us. We prefer not to acknowledge that something did happen. It did hurt. It was disappointing. It was embarrassing. It did cause anger. It did cause frustration. There is hate in our hearts towards those who caused the hurt. Denial is choosing to deny the truth and live a lie. The way you live a lie is by telling others around you, "I'm good," when you are not good. Or you have a dismissive attitude of "It's whatever," when it is not the case at all. It does matter. In the religious world, denial says, "The joy of the Lord is my strength," while holding on

to the unforgiveness which weakens the strength that joy can bring. Yes, that scripture is true, but in order to receive what God can give you, you must first give Him what ails you. "Where the Spirit of the Lord is, there is liberty" and there is freedom. Freedom comes from releasing, openness, and honesty. It comes from accepting the facts and not denying, ignoring, or lying about them anymore.

2. **Repression** – This refers to the memories we push down unconsciously attempting to forget. No matter how far you try to suppress those thoughts, they are ever so real and present in unanticipated moments. I'll talk more about this in the next chapter because certain instances can trigger unwanted or suppressed memories.

3. **Projection** - This is when you cast your thoughts or feelings onto someone else. Someone else's freedom exposes your bondage. For example, you do not like them, because, in your mind, you think they do not like you. They are secure in who they are, yet you think, they think they are better than you. This is foolishness. You project your insecurities onto other people when you are the one with the issue, not them. The truth is, they are not thinking about you to even talk about you, but because of that defense mechanism, you project your distorted view on others. And what ends up happening is that person can sense you have an issue with them and then they start thinking they did something wrong when they did absolutely

nothing. They do not even have a clue as to what happened, because it was all in your mind.

4. **Displacement** – This is when you direct your strong emotions, such as, anger or frustration on people who were not the source of that emotion. For example, if you are a boss, instead of addressing the issues you are having at home, you take out your frustration on your employees, because they may be less likely to react to you, based on your position. As parents, we can displace our unbalanced emotions on our children when it had nothing to do with them, not cleaning their room, for example. It could have stemmed from an argument with your spouse or a challenging day at work. Whatever the case, those moments of lashing out on the innocent can be detrimental to our loved ones, and not to mention the unhealthy display of irrational behavior before others.

5. **Regression** – This has to do with escaping the threat or anxiety of going back to a place in time you have moved past, "like children who wet the bed." For adults, a way of escape is procrastination, avoiding the task at hand, due to feelings of being overwhelmed by what is required of you. Some of us have challenges with losing weight. We think about the work required to lose those 10-20 lbs., after only one day of exercising and eating right. We can find it easier to return to our former state of overeating and sitting on the couch where it is most comfortable. The process of change requires effort

on your part, and it takes time. But this mindset will have you wanting to escape from the anxiety that comes with the "what ifs." "What if I fail? or What if I put all the weight back on again?" It is easier to go back to the place of defeat than to believe for victory.

6. **Rationalization** – This is when you explain the reason why you do what you do or react the way you react. There is a rationale behind your attitude issues. There is a rationale behind your lack of commitment. There is a rationale behind isolating yourself and keeping others from getting too close. These are the reasons that give you comfort and justify your unreasonable behavior. Others are not allowed to respond crazy or get upset, but you can because you feel you have good reason to be this way.

7. **Compartmentalization** – This is separating your life into different sectors in your mind so you can function without dealing with your anxiety or stress. You compartmentalize personal challenges such as alcoholism. There are some very skilled alcoholics, and drug addicts, you would never know had an underlying issue. They have mastered the ability to compartmentalize, so they can continue to function on a day-to-day basis. These are examples of "functioning addicts." They know they need to keep performing, so they keep their addiction hidden from others although they know they have deep internal challenges in their life.

Removing the mask forces us to go through a process of peeling away the layers. You cannot progress in life until you **go through** the process. The process does not feel good initially, but it is worth it in the end. This is not an easy route, but it is necessary. Keeping up with our many masks or defense mechanisms can stifle our movement. We are in the same place internally until we decide enough is enough. You must know it is vital to your growth and spiritual maturity to unveil yourself before God. And it is just as equally vital to disarm your defenses before those connected to your life. Why is this important? Because, when God frees you, then you are to turn and lead others to freedom. We do others a disservice when we are not our true, authentic, and unveiled selves.

TIME OF REFLECTION

Take some time to sit and write out those things that have caused you to wear masks, put up façades or hide behind defense mechanisms. Be honest with your emotions that arise and allow God to peel back the layers that have been your concealed weapons for far too long. Disarm and welcome God in your heart. This time of reflection will take some humility on your part, as pride will rise and cause you to "rationalize" why you need those defenses. The removal of your mask is a place of vulnerability, a place to choose to be naked and unashamed before God.

Ask yourself the following questions:

1. What are my defense mechanisms?

2. Which one is most prevalent in my day-to-day life?

3. How is this affecting my personal relationships? My relationship with God?

CHAPTER 4

Triggers

"Don't copy the behavior and customs of this world, but
let God transform you into a new person by changing
the way you think. Then you will learn to know God's
will for you, which is good and pleasing and perfect."
- Romans 12:2 (NLT)

Now that we have acknowledged something is beneath the surface to
be addressed, uncovered the hidden truth of the past, and unmasked
our defense mechanisms, we must now challenge the most important
factor of our journey...our thinking. Our mind is the place where the
hidden things are stored: in the deep-seated places of our memories.
And if not addressed and put in its proper place, these hidden things
can arise at any given moment and disrupt the emotional stability we
thought we had intact. Our memories are our memories. They are real
and those moments cannot be reversed. What happened did happen.

Nevertheless, we do have the means through the healing word of God to change how that moment in time affects our perspective and outlook of the liberty we have in Christ.

The Flash Backs

So, what is a trigger? A trigger is defined as "a cause (an event or situation) to happen or exist. It is typically a result of arousing feelings or memories associated with a traumatic experience." It is what sets in motion a chain reaction. A trigger brings about, stirs up, or rekindles an emotion from within based upon what is occurring without. In other words, a present situation can cause you to have a flashback. It is like a brief movie clip that plays in your mind of a past moment, causing those exact feelings to rekindle. As a result, you respond the same way today that you did before, based upon something that happened a long time ago. For example, when I would hear of similar violations happening to children in the news or I thought the same thing was happening to another child, in my mind I would go back to when I was nine years old. The current circumstance would cause the overflowing emotions of rage, hatred, animosity, and even dread to rise to the surface. I would detest those who caused me harm all over again. I would have so much indignation on the inside, it literally would paralyze me in that place of my memories. For years I was just stuck on an emotional roller coaster. I could not filter my thoughts properly, apart from the word of God.

Emotional Suppression

Triggers can be why some people flip out over the smallest things. The person's reaction had nothing to do with what just happened, but this encounter triggered an emotion that did not warrant that type of response. But if you take the time to evaluate that response, you will see it came from a much deeper place than words can articulate. Emotional suppression is what I did for years. These bottled-up emotions never go away no matter how hard one tries to suppress them. Eventually, they will erupt like a volcano and spill over on whoever pushes the right button. People who were physically or emotionally abused as children can fall into this category. They often have fits of rage from the memory of what happened to them and direct the root of that pain by reacting in anger to those closest to them by repeating the cycle. Let me take a moment to talk to those who may be currently experiencing these cycles. Along with the word of God and consistent prayer, I encourage you to seek godly counsel as this pattern of bondage must stop in your generation so that another generation will not suffer from the same hurt and pain. Believe today, that God can heal and deliver you from even the innermost painful places. There is nothing IMPOSSIBLE for our God to do! Believe only and know that recovery is available and waiting for you to embrace now!

Think Differently

The process of changing our thinking is not easy. Why? Because it first takes a deliberate choice to want to shift. As I stated before, we are shaped by our past experiences, so that means our thoughts have been conditioned to filter from either a good place or a negative place, a place of optimism or pessimism, a place of hope or hopelessness, or a place of assuredness or paranoia. This means it will require an exerted effort to reverse the debilitating years of poor thinking. We have to be willing to challenge every thought that presents itself and comes up against the knowledge of God. 2 Corinthians 10:5, says we are to be, "Casting down arguments and every high thing that exalts itself against the knowledge of God, bringing *every thought* into captivity to the obedience of Christ." (emphasis added) This means we must check every thought at the door. In my "Before Christ" (B.C.) days, I used to go to the club to get my party on, lol. Before getting into the door, the bouncer would need to check your I.D. to ensure you were age-appropriate, and that you were also wearing the proper attire for the establishment. If you did not meet the requirements, you were not permitted to enter. It's time to be a bouncer over your thoughts. If it is not age-appropriate thinking as a mature Christian that provokes a response worthy of God getting the glory, then that thought is not permitted to enter. It is time to decide if your mind will be an establishment in which the word of Christ dwells richly; where no matter what occurs in the surrounding atmosphere, if it is not beneficial to maintaining your level of freedom, it cannot enter your inward dwelling. It cannot wreak havoc and disrupt the stillness of the quiet, peaceful shores in your mind.

Life will happen without warning and events will take place that will trigger your memory, but if you continue to meditate and ponder on the word of God day and night, you will begin to see things from a different standpoint. Hebrews 4:12 (AMP) states, "For the word of God is living and active *and* full of power [making it operative, energizing, and effective]. It is sharper than any two-edged sword, penetrating as far as the division of the soul and spirit [the completeness of a person], and of both joints and marrow [the deepest parts of our nature], exposing *and* judging the very thoughts and intentions of the heart." It goes and separates that which is of God from that which is not. It cleanses and purifies the disgusting odor of foul thinking that produces unwelcomed actions. It causes you to see things through the lens of heaven and not the lens of this world. It will cause you to no longer see the people who hurt you as villains but see them as pawns in a plan bigger than them and bigger than you. When your thoughts are filtered from the mindset that this is not about me, but about God, then memories are no longer seen from the place of being a victim. They become testimonies of the victory.

Next Level Thinking

God gets the glory because what He predestined us to be, will still come to pass despite what the enemy attempted to do in my life and yours. When our thinking changes, the response to similar storylines is now not just to pray for the victim, but also the victimizer. As you renew your mind, you begin to generate thoughts from a place of overcoming rather than a place of devastation. Freedom comes from how we think about our past; when we no longer meditate on the trauma, but we begin to meditate on the purpose that came from the trauma. It is when we begin to apply the truth of Philippians 4:8 that says, "whatever is true, whatever is honorable, whatever is right, whatever is pure, whatever is lovely, whatever is admirable, if anything is excellent or praiseworthy, think on these things," then we can experience freedom. When you reach the place of freedom in God, your thoughts no longer dictate the actions of the old places, but you begin to think, live, and function from the new mind, which is operating with the mind of Christ. This is where love is your first thought, and the power of hate is diminished; where actions are produced from a mind of peace and not a mind of chaos because He keeps you in perfect peace as your mind begins to stay focused on Him. Every phase of the process is key. It is significant throughout each phase that you begin to take off the old self and put on the new self, by being renewed in the spirit of your mind. This means you must let go of your old ways of operating, old ways of reacting, and the old ways of seeing life through dirty lenses. It's time to change clothes, change from who you were, and step into the real you, with your new mind.

Decide today. Make the choice, "I declare and decree, I will no longer allow my past to dictate my emotional instability when life happens. I declare and decree, I have the mind of Christ!" Now, rejoice, for you have proclaimed victory over your mind and you are ready to continue your journey towards wholeness! AMEN!

A TIME OF REFLECTION

Challenge every thought that has held you captive in your mind. Allow God's word to address the memories that have triggered the emotional imbalance when certain events happen in your life. Then, start applying a new way of filtering each thought through the mind of Christ.

Ask yourself the following as you reflect:

1. Why do certain things trigger a negative emotion?

2. How could I have responded differently?

3. What scripture or scriptures am I going to meditate on to replace my old way of thinking?

CHAPTER 5

Purification Process

"So that the genuineness of your faith, which is much more precious than gold, which is perishable, even though tested *and* purified by fire, may be found to result in [your] praise and glory and honor at the revelation of Jesus Christ." - 1 Peter 1:7 (AMP)

I am sure by now you are probably saying, "This is too much. No more please. No more tears. No more exposing. This hurts too much!" Yes, I know exactly how you feel, but just a heads up...this is normal for the journey. It is necessary in order to evolve into your predestined position. As we grow, we are drawn to times of reflection, acceptance, and decision-making to reposition us to the other side of change. The key is to remember that the passage to God's destiny is not void of continual deliverances, tests, or trials. Everything we endure is a prerequisite to the ongoing process throughout our flight of life. We do not arrive overnight. We may heal in one area of our lives, but then look up and deliverance is needed in another area of our lives. Deliverance is like an onion with many layers that need to be peeled back in order to get to the source so we can have true freedom. Tests and trials are orchestrated by God to produce good fruit, good character, right motives, and pliability to lead us to the assignments He prepared in advance.

So, as you progress, I encourage you to practice surrendering to each step. Now that is easier said than done, which is why I said, "practice." "Practice makes perfect." It gets easier moment by moment. The more you are willing to relinquish control of your internal vices of protection, the more unfolding of your true self will be revealed - a person whom you could only imagine. But to get to that person, there needs to be some more purging, more cleansing, and more separation. You, my friend, must enter the place of refinement.

Refinement

What is refinement? Webster's defines it as " the process of removing layers, contaminations, defects, or impurities from a substance." It is the place of purifying and cleansing. It is the place of filtering and sifting. It is the moment of separation. This is the moment where God begins separating the profane or disrespectful things from our lives; the things that are not consecrated, blessed, devoted, holy, and the things that would cause a conflict to the call of obedience. These are things that are part of the flesh nature, the "want to do my own thing" nature, the things that are hostile towards the Spirit of God. Even after salvation, the desire to be in command is still ever so present within our flesh. Paul, said in Romans 7:15, "...For what I want to do I do not do, but what I hate I do." It takes a deliberate choice to go in the opposite direction of what our flesh is telling us to do. However, in order to reach the place of purpose, God must have full access to all of who we are: our minds, our souls, and our hearts. The measure of our surrendered heart dictates the measure of our ability to stay the course. The more we surrender, the more we are strengthened and equipped for the mission ahead.

...It's About Agreement

Tests and trials are meant to humble us. The humbling is so that we give up the inner battle and follow God. When we conform or adapt, we are saying we agree with God. In order for two to walk together they must agree. Now, to follow or come into agreement, we have to be willing to go in the direction of His leading. Disobedience and unwillingness to change caused the Israelites to wander in the wilderness for 40 years. I do not know about you, but I do not have another 40 years to waste. Agreement brings harmony, oneness, unity, and settlement. When we agree, we have peace. Believe it or not, there is a peace that you can attain that is beyond your understanding. You can literally be in the middle of so much confusion and drama, but inwardly be at peace. Yet, it is only attainable when you give up fighting, kicking against the bricks, and surrender.

Testing by Fire

As you yield, there is an invitation for you to accept and step into the fire. This step is where a death will take place: where all of you have to die. All of what made you - your environment, your trauma, your deliberate choices - all of it has to be examined in the fire. Now this place is not to destroy you, but it is to build you up so you can handle the unanticipated obstacles along the way. It is so you do not faint during the intense examination of your heart. Through this testing by fire, there are two things God will continually go after - disobedience and resistance. In case you have not figured it out...I have a newsflash for you!!! The closer you get to God, the more He turns up the heat!!! Yes, there is heat applied to bring everything that disrupts the flow of His Spirit in our lives and blocks our ability to be used to impact the lives of others. If certain attributes about us never change, then we become the barrier in someone else's life. We were meant to be lights in the midst of darkness, the salt of the earth, and atmosphere changers. We are not like the world, so we are not expected to act or think as the world acts or thinks. The ultimate purpose of the refiner's fire is to bring us back into position with God's original plan.

When gold is refined, it has to go into the fire. At the end of the process, the fire produces something elegant and cultured in appearance. Depending on the quality of gold, be it 10, 14, or even 24 Karat, each undergoes varying levels of intensity of heat. The better the quality, the higher the intensity. The intensity of the heat causes the gold to melt and the impurities start to separate and come to the top, and then they are skimmed or removed. We were created to be a reflection of God and to get the reflection He is seeking, the dross of our fleshly nature must be consumed and burned away by His flames of purification. God Himself is the one who sanctifies us to bring about wholeness and completion in our spirit, our soul, and our body. He is the one who is faithful and committed to do the work within us. He will not stop until the work is finished at the return of Jesus Christ. God needs to turn up the heat to bring up any and everything that is beneath the surface and is keeping us from coming into agreement with the purpose.

Yield to the Exposing

What is God exposing in the fire that you need to yield to Him? Is it fear? Remember, fear comes in many forms – fear of failure, of success, of rejection, of public speaking, of dying, of not having enough money, or even the fear of being broke again! Fear represents the lack of reliance and dependence on God. Fear can cause you to make rash and unwise decisions. Fear is tormenting, nerve-racking, causes sleepless nights, mental breakdowns, paralysis, and anxiety attacks that are often mistaken for heart attacks. Fear is a form of resistance. Fear is a stronghold that can grip you and stop you in your tracks. It literally can build an invisible bubble around you where no one gets in and you can't get out. The truth is...fear is the opposite of faith. Faith is the substance, the essence, the basis of things yearned or longed for and the evidence or proof of things not seen. This journey requires a foundation constructed and built on faith…faith that is unmovable, unshakeable, unaffected by delays and detours on the journey. Faith helps you stay on track.

Another area that God may be exposing is the need for acceptance. It is where you do things out of obligation, for the approval of others and where you seek the pats on the back for doing a good job. Doing things out of obligation or the need for approval is seeking for validation of self-worth. It affirms significance and importance. However, if you are not careful, it can plant seeds of resentment and disappointment. You can begin to resent those who constantly call on you to fill in all the gaps and feel disappointed if no one notices your efforts. Be sure everything you commit to doing is based upon the leading and prompting of the Holy Spirit. Seek God first as to where He would have you be if there is a need He has for you to fill. Let the approval come from God and not people.

Perhaps there is the need to give up the negative outlook you have about yourself. This is rooted in low self-esteem. Low self-esteem not only causes you to criticize yourself, but you also are very critical of others. This posture of heart is an indication that the filter of your lens needs to be cleansed so that you can see yourself and others through the eyes of God only. However, how we see ourselves is based on how we see God.

Still another area God may be exposing is what we speak out of our mouths. For example, venting and complaining is a clear indication that we have discontentment in our hearts. Even though good things have happened over and over, there is still dissatisfaction. This cannot remain or be a part of the place God is taking you. Our mouths are to speak from a heart full of life, faith, hope, joy, and peace. So, discontentment must be surrendered once and for all.

Stay in the Fire

The bottom line is the exposing is to correct what has gone unchecked for too long. Where God is taking you, there needs to be an activation of power, ease of movement without restraint, no hesitation, a quickness to listen, slowness to speak, and slowness to anger. There will need to be freedom to go where He says go, do what He says do, and say what He says to say. This all must be executed with boldness, power, and authority. This process of purification to bring balance and alignment in our thinking and to have the ability to "pause for the cause," is about progression and growth. This is not just about making us holy, pure vessels, but also ensuring we have the endurance to be able to stay the course. We have to stay in the fire long enough so that what is beneath the surface, in the core of our being, can rise to the top. The longer we stay in the heat, it can become unbearable, as the heat is meant to check for pure motives. The challenge can be the tendency to want to jump out of the fire prematurely when the power of the heat becomes agonizing. We oftentimes are so focused on the heat we missed the purpose of the heat. The purpose is to get us to die to the self-life. If you have ever witnessed the process of someone dying, it can be a long, exhausting, and painful process. Death can be instant without pain but dying can be a slow journey towards death. How we respond to the heat will determine how capable we are of handling the magnitude of the assignment. Nevertheless, just like Shadrach, Meshach, and Abednego, Jesus was in the furnace with them. They did not have to endure the fire alone. Therefore, God does not allow tests and troubles or hardships to occur in our lives, and not walk with us through it all. He is with us the entire time.

When I went through my own furnace experience, there were things that I did not realize were still so deeply embedded in my DNA. I had the misconception that if I forgave someone, that I did not have to love them as well. The reality of that is I had so much resentment stored up that it affected my willingness to not only love those who hurt me, but also affected my willingness to extend the same grace God extended to me, to others. I secretly still held my violators in contempt. I held them hostage for years and had no idea that I was resisting God; the One who was attempting to heal my broken areas. I also discovered I was still full of so much fear of rejection, failure, and worry about what happened to me could happen to my children and grandchildren. Fear caused me to second guess myself, seek the approval of people over the approval of God, and not allow me to move in certain arenas based on the disillusionment that I would not be accepted "as is." The times I spent in the Refiner's fire caused me to admit to some stuff. I was disappointed with God, that He did not rescue me as a little girl and did not prevent things from happening in my adult life. It was in this place where I came clean. I was no longer hiding my heart. I was ready to be vulnerable before Him. I was tired of being bound, tired of the cycles, tired of the pain, tired of being afraid, and tired of the memories that restricted me from being the woman He kept telling me I was in His presence.

Now, from the outside no one would know, as many of us tend to project or hide. I functioned like I was free, but on the inside, there was a constant battle going on. But, when the flame hit and things began to surface and I could no longer contain it, I had to make a choice to hold on to it or let it be removed, never to be seen again. This was my crossroad moment to go higher or stay in the valley, continue, or stop, to change or remain the same. In the midst of the heat, it is what I call a "now" experience. The pondering or mulling over we do when we have to make major decisions is not available or permitted when you are being tested by fire. It is a "now or never" moment. The choice you and I make in the "now" moment begins to activate what is needed to initiate the pruning process, so in the end, there is a bearing of fruit that will remain. This moment did not allow me to hesitate. I had to reflect on what He had been telling me all along. My eyes needed to open and see that God did not call me to walk in fear, but to walk in His power, authority, love, and stableness of mind. I had to meditate on His word that said, the opinions of man were a snare and a trap; that I am accepted in the Beloved; that He has not left me nor forsaken me. I had to see He was with me in the fire. I had to open up, surrender, and TRUST. Trust...whew...that word right there! I will talk in more detail later about trust, but for now, I will say this is why we resist so much. We do not trust our lives in the hands of the One Who gave us this life. And despite our lack of trust, He is still so good at taking His time in bringing us to the point where we say, "I surrender."

TIME OF REFLECTION

For this time of reflection, sit for a little longer than usual. It may take a minute to get to a place where you allow God to turn up the heat so the things that require purification for the journey can be revealed. Remember, these are things tied to your behaviors, actions, and even your motives - nything that can prevent you from coming forth as pure gold.

Ask yourself as you sit and wait:

1. What is God trying to show me in my character that is not in alignment with His will and His way?

2. What does He want to separate me from that is restricting or preventing me from exhibiting spiritual growth for the next phase of the journey?

3. What do I need to surrender in my "now" experience?

CHAPTER 6

Into the Deep:
The Place of Trust

"Fear Not, I am with you; Be not dismayed, for I am
your God. I will strengthen you, yes I will help you, I
will uphold you with My righteous right hand." - Isaiah
41:10 (NKJV)

Trust is such an easy word to flow out of the mouth, yet to the hearer,
it is extremely hard to comprehend and fulfill its required action. We
may trust someone a little bit, but if we are honest, we have one eye
closed and the other eye open to watch for any uncertain danger.
Some of us live by the saying, "trust, but verify." But my question
to that is, "if you have to verify, are you really trusting?" Well, it
actually depends on the track record in a relationship. If there was
a track record of trust developed and proven between two people,

then the consistency of that track record is verification in itself. In other words, if you have experience where God has shown that He is trustworthy through numerous difficult and challenging events, then there is no need to verify what has already been validated. So, trust is going to require you to go in faith and not by what you see or do not see. For there to be complete trust, our whole heart must be recklessly abandoned to the call, the beckoning, and the summonsing of His still small voice. In this journey to purpose, God is seeking a heart that will follow Him without hesitation, without concern, without second-guessing, and without reservation. This is the type of heart that says, "I'll go. Send me, even if I don't understand or don't have all the details...I will trust You, Lord."

Total Reliance

Trust at this level in the journey requires one to not think they have to have an answer to the problems set before them. There has to be a resistance to the desire to lean on your own understanding and your years of acquired knowledge and intellect. This type of trust involves going forth without knowing the next turn along the path. It is taking God's hand and letting Him lead you without a map or GPS in front of you. This path of trust expects you to acknowledge He is Your guiding light, and it requires you to affirm and reaffirm that He is the strategist of your life. He is the one who not only knows the plan, but He wrote the plan. He just needs you to get in position with the plan and let Him guide each step of the way. Along this journey, total reliance and dependence on God is a necessity. It is a necessity if we are to be representatives of the Kingdom of God. Remember, this is the purpose of why you were created. It was not about you reaching or achieving your own personal goals; those are just the by-products of you fulfilling the predestined call upon your life. In other words, there is no room for self-dependence, because if you check your track record, you will discover there were many bleeps and blunders that came with relying on self. There were times that you were in the driver's seat and you ended up back in the same place you started. You made a complete about-face. When we refuse to follow the one Who knows best, we can expect confusion, bewilderment, and misunderstanding.

Be Still and Know

Trust comes from a relationship with God that resides in peace, where our minds are fixated on Him and Him alone. It is birthed from the place of intimacy. You cannot trust anyone you are not intimate with or allowed to be weak, naked, and unashamed in front of without judgment. As you grow in oneness with the Lover of your soul, the walls of distrust come down, and the leaning and depending begin to commence. This is the place where we discover how to be still and know that He is God. It is here where we learn that He is the great I AM. The words "Be Still" come from the Hebrew word Raphah meaning, "be weak; to let go; to drop your hands; to release." It is translated to mean "cause yourselves to let go" or "let yourselves become weak," "become vulnerable or surrender." Now being weak is not something most of us desire to be or even want to appear to be in front of others. We all want to present a strong front as if we have it all together. This is a challenge for those who are strong-willed and unable to go with the flow **if** they are not in control of the flow. This is especially challenging if you are a resourceful person, someone who is skilled at making things happen at any given moment. The weakness of the strong-willed person is the fear of anyone ever seeing their imperfections or their inability to hold it all together. The misconception is that they see weakness as a flaw and a person who is vulnerable, as a pushover, thinking people are taking their "kindness for weakness." So, it is only natural to oppose or fight against being led into places of uncertainty. But as you become more acquainted with God's nature, His character, and His voice, you will be strengthened in your confidence of not only Who God is, but also Who He is in your life. At the moment of total vulnerability, He can then have a mature dialogue with you. In the place of trust, there should be quick obedience, because you **know** He loves you and you are certain that the direction He is taking you will not bring you harm. To "have a knowing," means that you come to recognize and perceive that beyond you trusting God, He now trusts you as well. You know He trusts you as you receive more responsibility. But more responsibility does not come until you move from your place of comfort to dwell and reside in the assurance that God is with you through it all.

Unchartered Territory

Trusting God completely, as I just said, requires coming into what I call, "unchartered territory." And believe me, it can be a little frightening. If you are like me, you may have asked yourself questions like, "Why am I so afraid to move forward? Why do I get to the edge of the water and stop? Why won't I go all the way in? What is holding me back? Why do I resist the tugging on my heartstrings telling me to let go and follow the Voice leading the way?" I do not know about you, but I had come to a place where I was tired of fear gripping me and holding me hostage. It kept me from discovering the beautiful oasis that awaited me beyond the place I call *The Valley of Stuck and Restricted.* I decided to take the step, trembling, and all, not knowing what distractions, obstructions, or challenges I would have to face and overcome. But, just like God told Joshua, I heard, "Be strong and courageous. Do not be frightened, and do not be dismayed, for the Lord your God is with you wherever you go." And know these are the same encouraging words that are being spoken to you today.

Respond to the Call

One day, I sat and wrote out what I saw, as it relates to taking the step as a response to His call for me to come. This is what I wrote: "As I visualize the vast, broad view of the ocean and there is no end in sight, I hear a voice say, 'come into the deep.' My heart is overjoyed initially because I hear the voice of the Father summoning me. But then I quickly become afraid. Why? You ask. Because I cannot see how far out, I am to go. There's nothing to keep me from drowning. What will I be able to physically hold onto? I remember Jesus telling Peter to come and when he saw the winds and the waves, he began to drown. 'Will this happen to me?' I ask. But then I hear Your voice again say, "trust, just trust Me. This is the place of total dependence. The place where your only guide will be My voice. If you can hear My voice, then you can trust the way."

And into the deep, I went, one step at a time. Was it easy? Absolutely not. Do I regret it? Not one bit! Because I sensed with each step, I not only saw fear fading away, but I saw confidence gaining up on my heels. It's in the place of trust that one learns true surrender. It's in this place that you willingly obey. It's no longer a "have to," but a "want to." You want to do what God asks of you because you now know and understand the love, He has for you is indescribable. So, with that, you are merely resting in the safety and loving arms of your King of kings and your Lord of lords, your Abba Father, Himself. So, I will end here with a poem I wrote in 2010 and revised in 2020, as I began my process of trusting. I did not realize it had been 10 years since I wrote this poem. The significance of the time difference is that 10 means "complete and perfect." It also signifies "testimony, law, responsibility, and the completeness of order." The Lord has truly completed and perfected some things in me and my own journey to purpose.

"Grow as I Go: Take the Step"

I'll grow as I go; I'll grow as I go.

I may fall on my face and make simple mistakes.

But, by Your grace, I'll grow as I go.

I launch into the deep, Oh, Lord quicken my feet.

I know I'm ready now, just show me how.

So, I take the step, with no regret.

Because, as I step, as I go,

Your faithfulness I have come to know.

You led the way, and my heart did not stray.

No need to lack trust, I know,

hand in hand it has been just us.

For two have now become one,

And this bond will never be undone.

TIME OF REFLECTION

Spend time in the presence of God and reflect on His track record in your life. Ask God to show you the times He was with you, when you did not even realize it at the time. Then, reflect on how much you have grown throughout the years and have overcome so much.

Now ask yourself the following questions:

1. Why do I allow challenges to keep me from taking the next step?

2. Do I truly rely on God completely? If no, why not?

3. Am I really ready to go and grow?

4. If yes, what am I willing to lose in the process?

CHAPTER 7

Point of Overflow

"The thief comes only in order to steal and kill and destroy.
I came that they may have and enjoy life and have it in
an abundance (to the full, till it overflows). - John 10:10
(AMP)

While we continue walking in our healing, surrender, freedom, and
trusting God with our whole heart, we encounter the moment of overflow, an overflow of love, joy, and peace! It is an overflow of God's
goodness that is immeasurable, unexplainable, and even uncontain-
able. This is the place of the abundant life that Jesus Christ died on the
cross for us to experience. He came so that I could be free from ALL
chains of bondage. He came so that I would evolve and become the
person He spoke over before I was a mere seed in my mother's womb.

Yes, there was a purpose to it all, to get to this place where we
are drawn into His presence, swept off of our feet, and submerged

in a river of living water. This is about being so saturated in a life of authentic grace and mercy that you no longer see through the eyes of this world, but you obtain a heavenly perspective that only the ones who come forth as pure gold get to experience. Oh, it is available for all, but only the ones who are committed, unwavering, and "tried and true," get the opportunity to experience the fullness of this joy that is freely given while sitting at His feet. I am not talking about basic Christianity. I am referring to the abundant life that turns you into a drink offering for the brokenhearted, where the well of living water springs out of you onto others. It is where everyone around you has a life encounter, and those who were once blind now see. It is when the impact of heaven meets earth through your life and God gets the glory every step of the way. This all happens when we reach the saturation point.

What is the Saturation Point?

The saturation point is when nothing else can be added, received, or accepted. It is the point of being filled, full, or brimming over. When there is a heavy rainstorm for days at a time, the rivers can begin to overflow their banks and then start to flood the surrounding land. Oftentimes if an area is already below sea level it is most likely prone to floods. For example, the city of Annapolis is susceptible to flash floods anytime there are long periods of rain. When this happens, it can become extremely dangerous at a moment's notice. Since the flow of the waters can cause so much damage to everything in its path, it is imperative that people take precautionary measures to protect themselves and their property. Unfortunately, people often underestimate the hidden danger by attempting to drive through the high waters that have flowed into the road. They attempt to drive through and unbeknownst to them, their car becomes engulfed, is swept away, or becomes stuck and they are unable to reach their intended destination. The occupants must be rescued, and some are rescued just in time.

Pouring Out

That form of overflow can be compared to living a life of disobedience, rebellion, and resistance to God's perfect leading. This may have been the place where you were prior to this chapter, but I pray by now that you have allowed the debris, the obstructions, and the hidden things to be cleaned out and removed by the power of God's healing presence. I pray you are now beginning to experience the flow of the river of living water moving on the inside, bubbling up to flow on the outside. This is the focus of the point of overflow I am referring to.

It is the point where we pour out onto those who we encounter. The pouring out of God's Spirit in our lives is for our benefit, but it is also to benefit others. Remember this journey to purpose has always been about the purpose God prepared, pre-planned, and predestined when you were created, so it is all for the building of His kingdom here on earth. People come to know the one, true living God through your life. You are the first Bible that many people read to reveal the

Savior. When we humble ourselves under His mighty hand, He comes in to take up residence on the inside of us. With each step we take to be overcome by His presence, then the more of God's presence can flood our heart and mind. We then come into alignment, into oneness, with one focus, one purpose, and an unwavering heart to do His will and to please Him with every fiber of our being. So, when God needs a blessing to take place in a person's life, you are now open and willing to do whatever He asks of you. There is no longer resistance to His call to "love My sheep." The pouring out of His love into your heart changes you to where you find delight and joy in partnering with Him to be a blessing and no longer a hindrance. To get to this point, there must be an outpouring of His Holy Spirit, to the point of overflow. You will not be able to move in the things of God without the fullness of His Spirit. It is through the help of the Helper that your heart will be moved in such a way that you can love others the way God has loved you. God's love is unconditional and His greatest mission for us is to demonstrate that same unconditional love to all. To do this you will need either an infilling or a fresh infilling of the Holy Spirit for the gospel to continue to reach the uttermost parts of the earth.

Infilling to Equip

Imagine a large clear pitcher with a handle on the side and it is full of clear, refreshing water, waiting to be picked up and poured into the empty glass sitting beside it. The pitcher has no lid, as the pitcher will need to be refilled if more empty glasses also need to be poured into. The pitcher can never be empty as its purpose is to continually pour out what is inside into the empty glasses that need refilling again, and again, and again. This visual serves a two-fold purpose. The pitcher represents the Holy Spirit pouring into you and me who are the glasses. But the pitcher also represents you and me who pour out the love His Spirit has deposited within us to those around us who are now the glasses to be filled.

We need the infilling of the Holy Spirit who is our Helper, to teach us all things and bring everything to our remembrance. If we are in tune with the Holy Spirit, then we will never forget nor abort the mission. He will continually remind us why we must keep going when we want to throw in the towel. When all around us is falling apart and there seems to be no hope in sight, Holy Spirit is the one who says, "You can do all things through Christ who strengthens you. Keep moving and fear not, for the I AM is with you. He goes before you and He is with you." In your moments of weakness, He will help, because no matter how much you think you know or how much you claim to pray, there are times in this journey when you are speechless and cannot muster up the right words or even know what to ask for in prayer. However, Holy Spirit knows what to intercede for on our behalf, with prayers that are too deep and too intense for words. He can interpret my innermost feelings and the things I can't articulate or put into words…He gets it! Jesus! That right there gives me such great comfort and joy, that when I cannot even pray for myself, I have an Intercessor that can pray me through better than any person I could think to call upon.

It will behoove us to acknowledge the gift given to us to walk us through the path of righteousness. The Holy Spirit is a person. You have to acknowledge Him, as I said before. He was given to us to Help us, to guide us, and to lead us into all truth. The Holy Spirit is the gift bearer. Now, imagine having a house guest come to visit you bringing gifts. Someone else opens the door and lets the house guest in. You are so busy preparing for the guest and getting everything ready around the house, that you never go to greet your guest to receive the gifts the guest has for you. If you stop for a minute, acknowledge the intricate part that Holy Spirit plays in your life and recognize you NEED the gifts given to operate and function at a higher degree of anointing that is upon your life, then all the busyness and doing everything within your own strength will cease and desist. There is peace when we learn how to get in the flow of the Holy Spirit.

Stay in the Flow

Once we get in the flow, we must remain in the flow of the Holy Spirit. Ephesians 5:18 says, "we are to ever be filled and stimulated (*engaged*) with the [Holy] Spirit." (AMPC) (emphasis added) Engagement is activation. You cannot activate the Holy Spirit in your life if there is no relationship and no acknowledgment that He is a present help for you daily. There must be a yielding and a surrendering for there to be an activation. To stay in the flow, you must activate the flow. This activation is cultivated when there is a constant flow of oneness between you and God's Spirit.

Staying in the flow is remaining in a place where you can become so drenched and soaked, that you are dripping wet from spending quality time in the presence of God. To soak is to allow something to be thoroughly immersed, submerged, or completely wet by a liquid. This can only happen by staying in constant connection and communion with God daily. Being submerged is significant because it is in this place we are changed. It is where our thoughts, behaviors, and actions are no longer our own, but completely come under the influence of Holy Spirit. Staying in the flow is keeping your heart in a place where you can be led, be at ease, rest, and follow. When we take the time to build ourselves up in our Most Holy faith, by keeping ourselves in the "love of God," as Jude 1:20-21 talks about, then we are strengthened in our faith. The doubt and wavering back and forth begins to diminish, and the confidence of the Lord propels us forward. But, let me make it clear so there are no misunderstandings. Being in a relationship with the Holy Spirit is not a feeling or some display of jumping around and gyrating all over the place. This is an inner connection, an experience between you and God that is indescribable. YOU MUST have an encounter with the Holy Spirit for yourself. This requires a hungering and thirsting for all of God. You know you are in the flow and have had an encounter when you no longer see, think, or act the way this world does; when you go in the opposite direction of what your flesh wants to do. If I can give an example, it would be when I came to the point where I could have unconditional love for those who violated me; the ones who the enemy used to try and stop the potential power that would be released through me to impact the lives of so many. When I grew in my relationship with God, He not only healed my heart of every memory, but He gave me a new heart; a heart that can only be restored when you soak in His presence. You must soak, soak, and soak some more until you are dripping wet with His presence; until He changes your appearance. Imagine yourself as a clear glass of water and He is the drop of red food coloring that falls into the water. The entire glass of water begins to take on a whole new look and it begins to look exactly like the red food coloring that was deposited.

This is what it means to be saturated with Him and Him alone. Until you reach this point, you will not be able to experience the abundant life Jesus came to give all of us. You will not be able to experience the full transforming work of the Holy Spirit in your life. There is so much more to experience in this journey, but without accepting the guidance and leading of the Holy Spirit, unfortunately, you will miss it every time, with your attempts to do things in your own power and strength. So, I encourage you this day, welcome the Gift Bearer and receive the wonderful gifts He has waiting for you to unwrap as you allow yourself to experience the point of overflow.

TIME OF REFLECTION

Take time to study and meditate on the scriptures about the person of the Holy Spirit. Take the necessary time to sit and welcome the Holy Spirit into every area of your life. Allow God's presence to overwhelm you with an indescribable kind of love so that you can reach the point of overflow and saturation.

Here are a few questions to ask yourself and ponder upon:

1. Am I at the point of overflow in every area of my life?

2. Have I unwrapped the gift of Holy Spirit in my life?

3. If I have unwrapped the gift, is it fully seen and received by others?

4. Am I spending enough time soaking in God's presence to allow my landscape to fully change?

5. If not, why not?

CHAPTER 8

The Finishing Work

"For I am confident of this very thing, that He who began a good work in you will perfect it until the day of Christ Jesus." - Philippians 1:6 (NASB)

The word *perfect* means, "having all the required or desirable elements, qualities, or characteristics, as good as it is possible to be. It means free from any flaw or defect in condition or quality; faultless; blameless." This has been the destiny of your journey: to get to the place that is deemed blameless and without flaws. It is where you see what He sees: a replica in His image and likeness, a willing vessel that He can trust with the secrets that are discussed in the secret place, and an ambassador or official representative of the Kingdom of Heaven here on earth. Yes, this has all been to finish a work that started long before you were even placed in the environment that *thought* it could shape and mold you. Not so my friend. There was great discussion in the heavenlies about you and who you were to become. It is so beyond what you can think or imagine, and it is great!! So, let us continue to see how this story ends and begins.

He Knew Me

God told Jeremiah, "Before I formed you in the womb, I knew you; Before you were born, I sanctified you; I ordained you prophet to the nations." Now you would think Jeremiah would be like, "Wow, really! That sounds so exciting!" I mean to know that the God of all, the One Jeremiah had been serving and worshiping his entire life, had just given him such a great mantle to carry. As a prophet to the nations, he was being appointed to be a mouthpiece for God. To speak on God's behalf is MAJOR!!!!! But, if you are like Jeremiah, like most of us are, you start to point out all of your limitations and why God cannot possibly choose you to do such a great thing. In Jeremiah's case, he felt he was too young for such a great task. However, God already knew his age, just like He knows every limitation you could list as to why God should not choose or use you. This initial reaction is normal. However, when you have confidence in the God who not only formed you, but sanctified, consecrated, and set you apart BEFORE your parents got together, like Jeremiah, you accept and embrace it because you know God is the Author and Finisher of your faith. He knew you then and He knows you now. Only people with whom you have an authentic relationship know you. Some people *think* they know you, but only those who see your heart truly know you. Only the one who really knows you and has seen your hurts, pain, imperfections, issues, hang-ups, mistakes, inconsistencies, and through all of that still believes that you are someone special and worth loving, is God Himself. God is the only one who sees all of it and still produces greatness without measure. He is determined to bring you to the place of transforming perfection, a sight to behold, a vision of beauty, and a complete masterpiece of His handiwork.

New Creation

My favorite scripture is 2 Corinthians 5:17, "Therefore, **if** anyone is in Christ, the new creation **has come**: the old has gone, the new **is here**!" (emphasis added) This has become my life scripture. Once I grasped the meaning of "if," which is based upon a condition that once I accepted Christ and made a commitment to live for Him, I became a new creation in that moment. With this discovery, the process of seeing the manifestation of this new creation meant I had to allow Him to do a work on the inside first before the evidence of that work could be seen on the outside. For years, the Lord showed me through the analogy of the butterfly's stages of transformation, what I was experiencing, and what He was producing privately before being presented publicly.

The butterfly goes through four stages of metamorphosis. The first stage is where an adult butterfly lays an egg on the leaf of a plant. When it hatches, it enters its second stage in which it becomes a larva also known as the caterpillar. Caterpillars do not stay in this stage long, but in this stage, all they do is eat. Caterpillars need to eat as much as possible so they can grow quickly. When a caterpillar is born, they are extremely small. However, when they start eating, they immediately start growing and expanding. Their skin does not stretch or grow, so they grow by shedding the outer skin known as molting. While they are growing, they are shedding their skin several times throughout this stage. The third stage is called the pupa or chrysalis stage. When a caterpillar is done growing and has reached its full length and weight, it forms the pupa. Now, on the outside of the pupa, it may appear as if the caterpillar is sleeping or resting, but in fact, there is much activity taking place on the inside. On the inside of that pupa, the caterpillar is experiencing some rapid changes. The caterpillar started out small, short, and stubby, with limited mobility. However, in the chrysalis, **the old** body parts of the caterpillar are undergoing an extraordinary transformation, called metamorphosis. The tissue, limbs, and organs of a caterpillar have all been changed by the time the pupa is finished. The final stage is the adult butterfly. When the butterfly first emerges from the chrysalis, the wings are soft and folded against its body. This is because the butterfly **had to fit all its new parts *inside* of the pupa**. Once the butterfly comes out of the chrysalis, it will start to pump blood into its beautiful wings so they can fly. Once the butterfly masters flying, then it will begin the search for a mate to reproduce and so the cycle for new butterflies begins once again.

If you have been wondering, these are the stages we all go through at various times in our lives. Perhaps after reading this book, you see yourself at stage one, but no worries, the hatching has begun. Or maybe you are at stage two and you need to eat some more of God's word and get more understanding of who God is and what He is doing in you. This is key to grow and shed the layers of self that prevent the next stage which I believe is crucial to your complete metamorphosis. Why? Because stage three is the stage of death, where the denying of self takes place. It is the place of purification I talked about in Chapter 5. Before you can evolve into the new creation that you have only envisioned in your thoughts, the old you must completely die. You must die for the new you to emerge into the "fearfully and wonderfully made" creation that God foreknew from the beginning of time. Now, if you are in stage four, then it is time to get comfortable with your new body, your new abilities, and spread your wings so that you can fly. It is time for you to come out of your shell, step into your greatness, and let your light shine! You are like a city set on a hill that cannot be hidden! Shine baby shine!

Bold as a Lion

Once the acceptance and the embracing of the transformed you have taken place, then operating in the power and authority given to you shall commence. There is no room anymore for second-guessing who you are after you have emerged from your chrysalis. The old ways of how you viewed yourself were left in the cocoon. Now you must function from the premise of where God has ordained you to be. No one called you to the place of useability but the Creator Himself, the Alpha and Omega, the Beginning and the End, Elohim, Yahweh, your Lord God Almighty. So, if He called you, then He equipped you to do the impossible, the unthinkable, the unheard of, and the unimaginable. Two examples come to mind: young David and the prophet Elijah. Both encountered situations where God would show Himself mighty and strong. Both had an assurance of who their God was, and they knew they did not need to fear any opposing forces. Both were put in positions for all to see who the One true living God was and for those who doubted, to come to know that He was real. God will also place you in situations that will cause the boldness of a lion to come forth. It may catch you by surprise initially, but the more you exercise your faith muscle, you come to know that nothing and no one is bigger than your God. And just like when David proclaimed to Goliath, that he came in the name of the Lord of hosts and the God of the armies of Israel, you too will go forth and all you will need is His name. Walking in boldness comes when you see the enemy entrenched in the lives of those whom God loves. And when you remember where you were and what you had to overcome, then the warrior in you will rise and you will stand for righteousness, bold as a lion.

Embracing True Identity

The finishing work is about changing your perspective, embracing your true identity in Christ, and living out the purpose that was beneath the surface the whole time. But for you to see, some things needed to be cleared out of the way. Each phase, stage, and encounter have all been designed to bring you to this moment in time. This has been about getting you to the moment that God has been waiting for you to reach. He knew every twist and turn you would have to go through to get you here, and it was worth the wait. Ecclesiastes 3:1-8 puts it this way, "there is a time for everything, and a season for every activity under the heavens: a time to be born and a time to die, a time to plant and a time to uproot, a time to kill and a time to heal, a time to tear down and a time to build, a time to weep and a time to laugh, a time to mourn and a time to dance, a time to scatter stones and a time to gather them, a time to embrace and a time to refrain from embracing, a time to search and a time to give up, a time to keep and a time to throw away, a time to tear and a time to mend, a time to be silent and a time to speak, a time to love and a time to hate, a time for war and a time for peace." (NIV) Every step you have taken has a time frame associated with it and only God knows when that appropriate time is to embark. It is not a moment too soon or too late. It is right on time.

In 2018, I had a vivid dream where I was being led to all these different tables where people I knew were sitting, but I could only visit. I was not permitted to sit at those tables long. There was nothing wrong with those tables, but each time I was summoned to keep moving on, because there was yet another destination. As the dream was nearing the end, I was now outside and saw a building encased in black glass. You could not see what was going on the inside of this building. Outside the building, there was a woman who appeared to be a concierge and she was holding the handle of the door beckoning me to come. I remember thinking, 'Where am I going and what is behind the door? as I was not able to see anything before stepping inside the doorway. When I accepted her invitation, I got to the doorway and saw waiters dressed in black standing behind the most beautiful table, set with fine china and gold candles set in gold candelabras upon a gold tablecloth. There was beautiful music being played from a harp. I looked up and saw some of my friends on the second tier getting food from a buffet. The buffet was elegantly laid out and any type of food you can imagine was on it. All of a sudden, I began to weep deeply as I stood in that doorway. I looked down at my clothes and felt so underdressed. I was not worthy to be invited to such a beautiful place. Then, I heard the woman say "It is okay. We have been waiting for you and you are welcome here." I share this so that if any of you, who after reading this book feels you are not worthy of all God has placed before you, know that if you were not, you would not have come this far in the journey. You too are welcome here. Your true identity is royalty. You are chosen and are equipped for the task at hand. Just like you needed me to speak into your life, others are waiting for you to speak into theirs.

I pray that as you begin or continue your journey to purpose, you will become a radiant butterfly, that is eager to meet with your Mate, your Prince, Your King so that together you can partner in the reproduction of more butterflies.

Go forth and make an impact…lives are depending on your next step.

TIME OF REFLECTION

I charge you to declare and decree from this day forward that you are a "New Creation." This is the time of embracing, so ask God to reveal the "new you" to you first. Ask Him to give you visions in your dreams of what the "bold and confident you" looks like. Now, I will say, you may cry a little when you see who you were created to be in the secret place. But then there will come a smile that beams from a heart of love and joy as you recognize God has done a work in me.

Final questions to ask yourself:

1. Am I willing to allow God to finish what He started?

2. Have I ever seen myself as a new creation? If no, why not?

3. When God reveals the "real me," will I accept what I see, or will I remain in my cocoon?

4. Do I have a strong conviction of who God is in order to walk bold as a lion?

Final Thought

As you continue in your journey, you will discover that God is a Promise Keeper. Everything He has spoken over you shall come to pass. David said it this way in Psalm 138:8 (TPT), "You keep every promise you've ever made to me! Since your love for me is constant and endless, I ask you, Lord, to finish every good thing that you've begun in me!" Let that be your declaration in your new beginning: "Lord finish every good thing that you've begun in me!"

Just so you know, there was a purpose behind why this book had only eight chapters. This is because "8" represents new beginnings. If this book has stirred something on the inside of you, guess what? Today can be the first day of your new beginning! With God, each day is a new beginning of learning more about who you were created and called to be in life: an "Atmosphere Shifter." You are a person who was purposed to make a difference. You are meant to be a partner in Kingdom building. You were born for this! Now, let go and let God, so you can enjoy the rest of your journey towards destiny!

An Invitation

If you are not saved, meaning you have not accepted Jesus Christ as your Lord and Savior, and after reading this book you want to experience the beauty of a relationship with the one Who died on the cross just for you, I invite you to read Romans 10:9 –10, (NIV) "If you declare with your mouth, "Jesus is Lord," and believe in your heart that God raised him from the dead, you will be saved. For it is with your heart that you believe and are justified, and it is with your mouth that you profess your faith and are saved."

Now pray this prayer with me:

Father, I proclaim with my mouth that Jesus Christ is my Lord and Savior. And I believe in my heart that He died and rose again from the dead to save me. I turn away from a life of sin and all of its devices. Today, I embrace my new life in Christ. I am a new creation because I am now in Christ, and my old life has passed away. In Jesus' name. Amen.

If you have already accepted Christ in your life and are a born-again believer...To God be all the glory!!!

But, if you desire to recommit your life to Jesus, I invite you to pray this prayer with me:

Abba, Father, Lover of My soul, I come before you this day to surrender again my will to Yours. I recommit my life back to You. Today, I ask you to forgive me of my sins. Then, I ask for You to create in me a clean heart and a renewed spirit within me. I choose Your will and Your way over mine. I choose to live a life submitted to You and You alone. I am a new creation because I am now in Christ, and my old life has passed away. In Jesus' name. Amen.

References

Ankarlo, Kris. "Water Rescue Team Explains Why and Where the Potomac River Is Dangerous, Deceptive" *Washington CBS Local,* 19 June, 2015

Bible Study. "Meaning of Numbers in Bible" *Bible Study* https://www.biblestudy.org/bibleref/meaning-of-numbers-in-bible/introduction.html

Domen John. "Anacostia River through Monday's storm" WTOP News, 11 July 2019. https://wtop.com/dc/2019/07/upgrades-to-citys-sewer-system-helped-anacostia-monday/

Holland, Kimberly. "10 Defense Mechanisms: What Are They and How They Help Us Cope" *Healthline,* 11 February, 2019. https://www.healthline.com/health/mental-health/defense-mechanisms

Learn About Nature. "Butterfly Life Cycle/Butterfly Metamorphosis" *The Butterfly Site*. https://www.thebutterflysite.com/life-cycle. shtml

Merriam-Webster Collegiate Dictionary. Since 1828. https://www.merriam-webster.com/

Thornton, Laura L. "Potomac River Placid Surface Deadly Currents" *Patch*, 2 July, 2013. https://patch.com/maryland/ potomac/potomac-river-placid-surface-deadly-currents https://washington.cbslocal.com/2015/06/19/water-rescue-team-explains-why-and-where-the-potomac-river-is-danger-ous-deceptive/

About the Author

Rev. Anita Proctor was born and raised in Capitol Heights, MD, and attended Ashford University where she received her Bachelor of Science degree in Business Administration. In 1997, she accepted Jesus Christ as her Lord and Savior, and in February 2009 accepted her call to public ministry. Rev. Anita was licensed to minister on October 3, 2014 at Cornerstone Peaceful Bible Baptist Church, Upper Marlboro, MD.

She currently serves as the Ministry Leader of the Intercessory Prayer Ministry (P.O.W.E.R.) and the Young Adult Ministry (G.A.P.). She also serves as the G.A.P. Sunday School teacher. She has served as a Conference speaker, Youth Leader, lead Intercessor of the Healing Rooms Ministries, and an active member of the Women's Ministry of CPBBC (W.O.R.D.). She is a Section Chief with the Department of Treasury, Internal Revenue Service with almost 30 years of Federal Government service.

Rev. Anita has been considered "a scribe" by her peers in ministry. She loves to capture in writing what the Lord is speaking moment by moment. She truly has a deep love for God and soaking in His presence. Rev. Anita carries a deep burden in her heart for others to overcome obstacles, be delivered and set free from rejection, fear, and the opinions of man. She is a "gap filler" always interceding for the lives of the lost, hurting, overlooked, and forgotten.

Rev. Anita has experienced for herself how the power of God can literally change a person's life. In February 2004, she joined Cornerstone Peaceful Bible Baptist Church, where her life has been completely transformed for God's glory, and she has never been the same. Her favorite scripture is 2 Corinthians 5:17 which emphasizes that anyone united with Jesus gets a fresh start and is created anew from the inside out!

Rev. Anita is married to her high school sweetheart, Brian "Keith" Proctor. They have two beautiful daughters, Keishawna Renee' Simmons and Jocelyn Marie Proctor; an awesome son-in-law Michael J. Simmons Jr.; a special bonus daughter, Sherrie Wright; and three beloved grandchildren, who are her pride and joy, Xavier Simmons, Aurora Simmons, and Jeremiah Ransome.